Echidnas Don't Live Here

Also by Belinda Broughton and published by Ginninderra Press

Sparrow: Poems of a Refugee
A Slip of the Tongue
Not Looking For Signs

Belinda Broughton

Echidnas Don't Live Here Any More

Poems of loss and recovery
since the Black Summer bushfires

Acknowledgements

My loved husband and rock, Ervin Janek; my children and their families (especially the architect!); Alex from Barnard constructions (best builder); my new friends, fast becoming old friends, from our support group In This Together; the staff at the Lobethal Recovery Centre, especially Tina Benbow (I know it was your job, but even so!); all who helped us in any way at all, so many, so many; everyone who gave anything at all, from T-shirts to shovels, to their time and work, to their shoulders to cry on, to money, to their good hearts; everyone who helps anyone in need, anywhere, at any time (this is what makes us human).

Graham Rowlands (editor extraordinaire); Margaret Wilson for proofreading; Rachael Mead for being fantastic; Hills Poets for their support, love and feedback on so many of these poems; Stephen Matthews from Ginninderra Press.

Melinda Rankin and René Strohmayer at Fabrik Arts + Heritage, for their support and for the opportunities that led to 'Edges' and 'Imagine Living on Nectar', the latter of which was written for *Flocking Together*, a moving image community artwork created by illuminart Australia and collaborators, projected onto the facades of the old Onkaparinga Woollen Mills (further details: www.flocking.illuminart.com.au); the team at illuminart Australia for the opportunity to work on this project.

Dedicated to Nature. May it soon make a lie of the title.

Contents

Preface

one day your life is quite normal, the next it burns down

before fire: innocence
after fire: it's too early to say

echidnas don't live here any more
each plant is worshipped
each returning bird is champagne
each animal is welcomed like a returning hero

in the fire-scarred land, we are all returning heroes
returning from the place of limbo
from bardo
the space between death and life

this new life has new houses, all gleaming and sterile
that need new memories, laughter and delight
to be impregnated into their walls

personally? I collate this book to put a line under all that
perhaps it is possible
perhaps not

On 20 December 2019, a fire began five kilometres from us, burnt southwards, burnt miles that way then turned and took the district. We came back next day to nothing. Everything we owned, apart from what we grabbed in the half hour before we ran, was burnt. Our home, studios, all our artwork, the trinkets of memory and love, our beautiful little pocket of bushland.

Over seventy homes were destroyed in our fire ground

alone. The details of loss to people and nature are appalling. I will not go into it further here.

Thus began our road to recovery: the trauma of loss, both material and mental, both human and natural, the mind-bending exercise of recreating a place to live, on land we loved.

We were lucky compared to most. Our daughter was two university subjects from being a fully qualified architect. She designed our new home, and managed the build. A loved young friend who has been building things for us since he was twenty did the building.

The recovery was complicated by Covid 19, which began affecting South Australians in March 2020, creating a time of great stress in which we had to physically distance ourselves from each other. I can't tell you how many people wanted to hug me through this time to make me feel better. Or how many I wanted to hug. Because, of course, we were not alone in this fire recovery trauma. Our whole community felt it, even people who had lost nothing.

Lucky or not, it is a long and difficult road. And it is not finished when you move into your sparkling new house. Trauma is a slow thing to recover from. Eventually, the good things of life need to replace the old. Somehow, you need to rewrite your brain. I stick my head under a rock about the latest war, and assemble this book from the writings since the date that my life burnt down.

Dragon's Breath

Cudlee Creek fire, December 2019

la   la   la
packing a few things
in the line of wildfire

erratic wind
with embers and ash
and birds, fleeing

to the west
the billowing smoke
of our undoing

my dead mother lights a candle
'there's not so much darkness…'
she says

crumpled buildings
the grandchild's face
is white with shock

from blackened trees
the charcoal lament
of crows

how the very air
hurts the throat
black lands

metal kitchen knives

standing to order
in the ash

how delicate
the thirty years of journals
in leaves of ash

inch ant
celebrating
any life at all

in the burnt lands
with eyes that are not wary
a kangaroo

dandelion
its face like a spring sun
first flower

Three lists

(written at two a.m., two nights after we lost Nearly Everything)

List of lost objects that matter now:
None of them

List of things lost that I'm sad about:
Bob the bird (shrike thrush) whom Ervin fed, and whom we loved.
All of the other birds, especially the small ones, wrens, thornbills, pardalotes, finches. Maybe the bigger ones got out?
Native animals, our resident echidna.
Ervin's sculptures and woodblock prints.
All of my on-paper haiga.
My hand-made paintbrushes and a couple of commercial brushes that still sang at forty years old.
The singing bowls. My shaman's drum.
All of Ervin's framed works and prints in boxes. A lot of his negatives. The ones I didn't scan.
My hut. His studio. Our little house in the woods.
The woods.
The records of our toys (that we made for a living for thirty years).
My jewellery, mostly worthless, but especially the ones made by friends. Ida for example. Her early student jewellery. She will never make it again.
My journals of thirty years. Drawings and raw poems that showed promise but never were transcribed.
A couple of my paintings.
The bird bath.
Ervin's tools, especially his chisels (some of which had been with him for fifty years) and his Japanese saws.
Other things that I will remember later.

Things to be grateful for:

Our bodies.

Our loved ones.

Our beautiful true friends.

The caring hearts of complete strangers.

That we have our computers, with the files of a lot of his photos and most of my poems.

That we have our car and van and most of our camping gear.

That sleep is usually easy for me. Even if it isn't tonight. It's two a.m.

That a lot of the bigger gum trees probably survived. That the beautiful bush will surely recover and we will watch it.

That we have a piece of earth that, in government records, is ours. That I have lived there long enough for it to be in my bones.

That I still feel connected to my dead son though I wish his corporeal body was sitting next to me.

Likewise, Mum and Dad. How unusual that they are with me tonight with their calm and graceful strength.

That my sweet loved man is as beautiful as ever. That he sleeps peacefully while I make lists.

That we do have resilience.

That nothing kills creativity.

That we will survive. And even, eventually, thrive.

I can't help thinking

I can't help thinking that we are in this situation precisely because we had something to lose, and my mind goes to all of the people who are sleeping on the street tonight, or holed up in a refugee centre, or running from world leaders' latest wars, or losing the very land they stand upon, the sea claiming it, all that salt water.

as if the world
prepared for this
I hold the ones I love

Baggage and Stuff

unfurling sunflower
my son's spirit whispers
on ashen wind

Our son Miklós loved sunflowers, and when he died, there were sunflowers at his bedside and sunflowers on his grave and sunflowers in the house for weeks. So when my granddaughter's sunflower begins to unfurl in the horrendous heat with such determination and resilience, and so soon after our latest disaster, it feels like a message from him.

Well, honestly, it feels like his warm hug is around me the better part of the time lately. And it looks like I don't need the physical symbols of his presence that I was keeping. Like the hat he gave me one day that hung, tattered straw, on the wall in my writing nook. It is gone and a lot of other stuff, that now feels like baggage, is gone.

lightness of being
the weight of Nothing
on my back

After I found out we'd been burnt out, I felt an odd lightness when I realised my possessions were gone. We keep things for weird reasons and attach stories to them. Was I possessed by my possessions? Were they an actual weight on me, that I now feel lighter? Already we have been given things that belonged to the deceased relatives of well-wishers. But these things arrive with a note that explains their attached grief. The oddest thing is, it changes the object to know, and suddenly we have a responsibility to care for the object. We feel a little heavier, and they a little lighter. Are we all insane? Or innately grief-stricken.

taking in the family washing
scent of sunshine

I was talking with Hana (my daughter with whom we are staying) about objects and the stories they hold. I said, 'I would like to have as little as I need,' and she said, 'You have as little as you need. You have three pairs of knickers and I do the washing twice a week,' and we laughed. I didn't tell her that her maths was shot.

What is it about knickers? How have they become the symbol of necessity? One has to laugh. Perhaps an ironic laugh, but one has to laugh.

from a stranger's
dead sister's
necklace
trinkets repurposed
on the Christmas tree

The complete stranger at the coffee counter

Her hard-luck story about how her son's dog destroyed her Christmas lights. I decide not to tell her my hard-luck story.

It's strange being in the midst of a trauma. It's like you are in some sort of weird bubble. You carry this darkness and no one else can see it. They go about their lives doing their ordinary things, worrying about their ordinary things like whether Chloe needs a second Christmas present because Crystal has two. And you look at them from your strange bubble and it just feels weird. They look as if they are not awake. Or as if they are so bound up in themselves that they have no connection to the outside world. You also know that was you three days ago.

It is surreal. I remember this from every trauma I have ever experienced. After a while, these feelings dissipate; already they are less strong. But then you meet some random person in a café who needs to tell you trivial problems and you see them, all the details about them, the colour of their clothes, the resonance of their voice and it doesn't, in any way, touch you. You nod and wait for your coffee.

her painted toenails
appear to have as much meaning
as the floor

scent of coffee
a man turns the page
of his newspaper

Like My Heart

like my heart
the cones
of *Xanthorrhoea*
both complicated
and simple
and surviving

During fires *Xanthorrhoea* (grass trees) are burnt to the trunks. The growing tips are left as cones showing that double helix pattern that one sees on pinecones. These cones begin pushing upwards immediately, and within days you can see the change. They often do well after fire, sprouting quickly, and within months they send up flower spikes that are taller than men. The plant itself is very slow growing. Most of ours were well over a hundred years old. Usually, they recover completely after fire, but the fires that day were so hot that more than half of the specimens on our place died completely.

broken heart
it's a medical condition
Xanthorrhoea

as if there was anything left

relentless summer sun
as if there was anything left
to burn

cutting wood
piling timber
a rabbit rushes out

small miracles
the perfect
standing spade

endless blue sky
and from charcoal and fallen leaves
first flower

pieces of
the five-hundred-year-old jug
its glaze still green

tears
they don't solve anything
fire fungi

through the counting
of losses
starlight

Earth Healing

after blessed rain
on burnt black earth
an orange jacket of fungi

Pyronema Omphalodes not only has a brilliant name, it is bright orange and only grows after fire. The fungi coat the earth with a sponge, binds it to the hills, and begins its rehabilitation. Our place hasn't seen fire for over thirty years. Where was it? Where were the seeds of *Kennedia Prostrata*, a prostrate legume commonly called Running Postman? I hadn't seen it growing for at least fifteen years, but it sprouted in millions and cloaked the earth with a carpet of green.

Within a year, there were very few bare spots. There was also a plethora of weeds, many troublesome but some, not only benign, but actively building soil, while native seedlings pushed up from underneath. My favourite is a type of dandelion that I quickly began to admire. So tough, so vigorous, and so beautiful. A carpet of tiny suns, all year. In the height of summer, the thistledown lies in pockets an inch thick. Will I be sorry I gave it its freedom? I am assured that it will begin to die out as the natives mature. But in any case I don't care, it is good for my heart. Also I have decided that of all the battles, dandelions are not to be one of them. The little piece of land we have will never be pure native bushland again. We damned Europeans are here to stay.

dancing barefoot
on earth that is in my bones
the crow's call

Red Heart

Sometimes I get so angry
with politicians for example
or people who are not yet changed,
who go about their business, about their lives
as if nothing has changed.
I am angry with those who do not allow
their hearts to feel or their minds to see.

I am angry with those who refuse to acknowledge
that this is but the beginning
that the world has turned
that the red heart has awoken
that the red heart is beating in anger
that the red heart is beating towards change.
There is no going back.
The transmutation has begun.
This is the lesson of fire.
Keep up, People.

There will be yet more suffering.
There will be yet more sorrow
but eventually your anger will be
as strong as mine
and you   will   stand   up.

You will stand up and the world
will stand up with you.
Our hearts will beat with fury.
The red heart will beat with ours
and there will be change.

We will stand together
ignited by anger and
ignited by love.
How can this not be so?
Love is the seat of our anger
and love will be our healing.

Love will be the sacred water
that drowns ineptitude
that, when the time is right
quenches the fires of rage
that brings us back
to our own beautiful, pumping hearts
that brings us back to each other
that brings us back to the earth
with its red and vibrant heart.

When despair grows in me

after Wendell Berry

When despair grows in me
about some past grief or future worry,
I rest in it a while, crying,
feeling impotent, and put upon.

Then I remember that old truth
about those worse off: the child
with the paper bones, or the man
who lost everything including his skin.

And I breathe in deeply.
I fill my lungs with air
that simply is.
It has no conception of good or bad.

And I notice that I stand in a world where
pigeons croon and peewits pipe their shrill note.
The earth is damp, the sun warm.
Children over the way squabble or laugh.

Despair sits behind me like a shadow
but I choose to face the light.

I draw with charcoal

I draw with charcoal
from my burnt home
what else can I do

The following poem was written before the fire for an art exhibition due to go up in February, nine weeks after the fire, in Lobethal, my local town and one in the centre of the firegrounds. The exhibition was called Solastalgia, which means the emotions one feels at the loss of loved environments. The exhibition went ahead, despite everything. As well as the poetry, I produced a thirteen-metre drawing on the wall of the gallery, using charcoal from our burnt place.

The poem was written for performance. I haven't changed it for the page. In view of the fires, I changed only two phrases.

Where the edges aren't

1

Who will speak for the trees? Who will speak for the trees?
Who will speak for the forest, for that part
of the natural world? Because, let's face it, it's all nature,
even this crass world with its concrete and steel,
its plastic paint and polluted pavements.
It   is   nature.

Can you sense that there is no divide
between one   and the next, between you
and the person standing next to me?

Can you sense that we are all just fragile bodies,
fragile bodies on a fragile earth
fragile bodies like your dog with his
welcoming eyes, or your budgie,
or the budgies in flocks of thousands out on the open plains?

Can you sense your sameness to the goldfish in your tank,
or the Murray cod with its ancient eye,
or the glint-eyed carp sifting mud and felling trees,
or the cormorant sunning its crucifix,
or the water it dives into.

Can you recognise that there is no divide?
The water it dives into: H 2 O, hydrogen, oxygen:
of what do you think you're made?
And carbon – carbon, the hard black stuff all over the hills:
of what do you think you're made?

Can you recognise that your body
is never still, not even at rest, that it is transpiring, breathing,
that air tumbles over your skin nor sure where the edges are
fractaling down to atoms, to energy, to pulse, to particles,
to waves, and water,   to waves and water.

You surface like a cormorant, the air
an accumulation of sky that you gasp, that courses
into your lungs, that blends with your blood, that becomes
you
that becomes
you.

You! even down to your bones –
bones in time, structure and poise,
calcification and decalcification,
replacing the gristle in a baby's hands,
in the hands of the old, all lumpy and protruding
even while the bones of their wrists break down before
the inevitable

the inevitable long time on the earth
friend of crows and ants and the sun
– bone time, long time,   bare-bone-truth time

Bare-bone-truth-on-decorative-shelf time:
a trinket collection of bones and shells
of the exoskeletons of beetles, of fishes' gill fans:
a reminder of what? That we die?

Or that we are made of earth,
of minerals excited by the energy of the sun?
We are made of plants with their chloroplasts streaming.

And what of this blue planet that we stream upon,
this blue planet turning brown?
What of the grey smoke of Australia?
What of our comfort, dependent on oil
on the dead remains of a million trees
that fed in the sun in long-ago geological time?

2

From where I sit I can see
the freshly cut stump of a tree.
It died this year. Its sap   stopped   flowing.
On the stump I can see all of the years of its life drawn in circles:
the years of its life, some fat, some lean, and finally
one year to finish it, or a dozen that got progressively worse.

My heart is in the heart of the tree, in its suffering.
My heart is in the heart of suffering: your suffering, our suffering,
the trees, the insects, the animals, the plants, the fungi,
all of those individual individuals, the ecosystems, the earth,
the delicate, beautiful balance of this   blue   planet,
this   blue   planet that we must   take   care of

that we must   take   care of
like a mother tends a baby
like you clean your fish tank or your lover's face
like you offer an arm to the frail
like you care for ones in pain
like you feed the starving and rescue
the stranded puppy from the swollen river
like you rescue
the river.

You rescue the river. You rescue the earth.
You rescue the air, the delicate layers of atmosphere.
You rescue the tiniest forms of life and the largest.
You rescue your brother, your mother, your grandchild's grandchildren.
You rescue the known, the ones of your blood and
you rescue the stranger on the street.
You rescue brothers and sisters of all skin colours.
You rescue the damaged child.
You rescue the tattered butterfly that is
beating its wings on the pane.
You rescue them.

You rescue them because…
you rescue them because
you have no choice

and you rescue them because
you have no edges.

You have no edges because
everything,
every   thing
every   single   thing

is you.

Covid Complications

Psychologists who deal with trauma say that three months after a disaster, it is good for a community to come back together and debrief. They say it is part of the process that eventually leads to healing. Instead, we had Covid lockdowns.

covid fear
I look at my hands

covid jigsaws
with pieces missing

Our situation was further complicated by having to distance from our daughter and her family, where we had been staying, because our grandchildren had symptoms. Luckily, it subsequently turned out that they were fine, but in the meantime, we packed up all our worldly goods and went to stay in our friends' shack in a seaside town seventy kilometres away. This was so generous.

in rock pools
starfish
social distancing

'he doesn't understand social distancing'
said the woman about her dog

It was a time of terrible stress, for the whole society, actually, but especially for me. I was exhausted after the art, poetry, and the move. We were in a town with no support network, miles from home, in a pandemic that none of us understood yet. I developed a sort of spastic tic in my breathing that caused me pain in gut and back.

After two weeks we moved back to our daughter's place in the city because our friends needed their shack for isolating. The grandkids had recovered from their sniffles, and it was good to come back to the arms of loved ones.

covid lockdown
silence surrounds
the easter moon

Pink Moon 2020

clean and clear
the indigo sky
wherein rides
a pink moon
as soft as autumn
as calm as centre
as centred as earth
as tethered as love
as silent as this suburb
now that the children sleep

Saturday night but no revellers
drink away their inhibitions
or fall into the arms of a stranger
no rapists, no prey
no police cars, no sirens
no wicked witches
no trolls under the bridge
no fat men eating money
no avaricious politicians

just the homely quietness
of a suburb in lockdown
under a pink moon
in an indigo sky

Broken Heart Syndrome

Sad on and off, sore in the upper chest and back.
I think it's a broken heart.
That's a thing apparently, a real medical condition.
This morning I wept for the loss of his artworks,
the ones I didn't scan or scanned so badly
that they will never again be prints.

Oh well.
And then I wept for the land, for
the silence there, the lack
of birdsong, cheeps and trills, the lack
of leaves, green and grey, the lack
of insects, and mushrooms, the lack
of habitat.

Oh well.
'Life goes not backwards nor tarries with yesterday.'
I forget who wrote that, it might have been me.
I've forgotten much.
The other day I tried to walk my mind
through the lost buildings of my life
looking for some insurance detail
but all I could see were my dead,
all I could see was what wasn't there,
not even faces
just the spaces in the air
where they could be but aren't.

Oh well.
I did not intend this to be morbid.
About now in a poem, I usually bring in
something delightful and put it on the page
to stave off bleakness. I thought perhaps
a dandelion with its brave tenacity
and face like hope.

After Loss

This thing, that thing,
things I made,
things to make things with,
things given, things loved
all gone, all gone.

Come now, come now,
there is no use to mourn,
there is no use to mourn.

Tomorrow the sun
will rise in the east
and it is fairly likely that you
will have enough to eat.
It is fairly likely that the rain
will be something to play in
and not an enemy seeping
through your clothes.
It is fairly likely that you
will have clothes.

It is also likely that during the day
you will turn your head and
see something or smell something
or hear something that
will open your heart.

You will feel it open
like the unfurling fist of a child
slightly painful at first
and then a rather large

feeling in your chest.
That is called 'heart-full'
and it only takes a small
spin on the earth to feel it.

So stop mourning now.
Be glad for what
is lost and what is gone.
Tomorrow the sun,
of course, tomorrow
the sun. It will rise
and the simple flowers
will open and so
will your heart.

Through gardens of kindness

for months
walking like a mummy
through gardens
of kindness

Living at our daughter's place was lovely actually, intimate time that parents rarely get, these days, with their grown children and their grandchildren. Very intimate given we were locked down together for months. We cooked and worked and gardened together and home-educated the children as well as we could. Hana bought two chooks, and we laughed a lot. Hana worked on the architecture of our new house. We had dreamed together but winter made it difficult.

In the meantime, the block had been cleaned. (Suddenly it was not called 'home' it was called 'the block'.) The South Australian government managed the fire recovery really very well (for the first year) with a centre in our local town. We were allocated a counsellor who helped us through the many problems, paperwork, documentation, grant applications (why do they make them so hard?), accommodation, and even things like furniture and blankets.

Our counsellor was called Tina and she was brilliant. One day she asked me, 'How is your apartment?' I said, 'I wouldn't exactly call it an apartment. It is a beautifully sealed shed with heating and cooling and a hotplate and a kettle. We have an en suite.' And I described how the 'en suite' was a nice sealed bucket for the nightly wees. I saw her face fall and thought, 'Actually this is not normal, is it?' But nothing is normal when you go through things like this. Within a week, a rental ten minutes from the block had opened up and it was allocated to us. A week later, a fridge and a washing machine were gifted to us!

all the good hearts
we will get through this
I tear my skin on a stick

this grant, that grant
we put our life back together
bit by bit

sadness and hope
like peel and fruit
in cake

Mother Pride

That wet form, bloodied and blotched
that opened its eyes on light while still
half inside my body, is a woman now.
She has two children, vital and lithe,
like will-of-the-wisps with substance.
She guides their eyes to make sense
of all this weird life and its stages,
moment by moment, braiding hair, kicking ball,
burying their uncle, this thing, that thing,
the things that change the course of a life.
We blunder through them, carrying our burdens.

Oh, Daughter, that's a good job that
you're doing there, the job of life.
And here I am. I'm meant to be wise by now,
but all I want, often, is my own mother.
And you, when I need it, even manage
to mother me.

A Little Time with Beauty

Tonight the crescent moon
was thin and perfect
north west at six p.m.

These details, who needs them?
Perhaps poetry feels obscure because
who cares about details of the moon?

Beauty cares; there is no doubt
Beauty cares.
Now, I'm not exactly sure who Beauty is

but I know her intimately as, I'm sure, do you.
Today we sat together as wind
ruffled the high branches of maples.

Leaves fell and fell and fell,
each of them in their own way
some floating, some tumbling, some spinning.

Between being one with the tree
and being one with the mulch,
each had its own moment of expression

its own brief dance.
Each had an individual
moment of intimacy with air.

Beauty and I sat there together
and afterwards
I felt a little lighter.

Lawn with Weeds

Parrots walk in the winter grass
stripping the early grain.

Herbs of various kinds
grow among the grasses.

We name them
'weeds'

but what I see there, is plant,
is earth pouring vitality into living tissue

is sunshine rattling around
in the green structures of cells.

Oxygen, water, earth, light,
the myriad dead things in the soil

I see plant, that amazing conduit
between earth and animal.

It vibrates with life,
is growing and growing

and never once
does it pass judgements

on humans
or call them names.

Morning Prayer with Blackbird

The blackbird has begun the business of the day
pecking, pecking, and wagging her tail.
Actually it's a male, black with a yellow eye
but they all look like females to me,
like busy widows. This one
is inspecting the potted plants for bugs.

Daylight pinkens the clouds.
I have come from my morning ritual
of singing the world to health.
That means you.
Yes, there is fear and there is disease.
Other people seem like a chemical weapon
but we still have eyes, and we still have hearts.
We stand on the same earth and
for better or worse, we breathe the same air.

Did you know that bits of your molecular structure
are right now zooming through me and mine
through you? It's all so much wholeness actually.
I send you good feelings. I send you love.
It doesn't feel like a hug but you can
take it and wrap it around yourself anyway.
It's warm and strong and it holds you
for as long as you want and no longer.

The blackbird feels it.
See? She lifts her head.

Winter Solstice

The dark time of year.
Odd things are black with frost
but, below bare trees,
the earth is sapping green.

Weeds spring in autumn here
when rain comes to seared ground.

With water as fresh as life
I take vitamin D and watch
the light change on this
cloud-spangled shortest day.

Perhaps I'll never again desire summer
when the hot winds swirl our fear with
tinder leaves, when plants roast brittle
and feed fires with tempers unheard of.

It's hard to celebrate all of that
but give me your fruit pudding
and your evergreen hope
and I'll deck them out
with paper stars.

Whisky Hour

A blackbird chitters in flight.
Most of us feel edgy at this end of day
with darkness looming.

Memories of tigers perhaps
send us scurrying for caves
send us scurrying for scotch.

'Scotch' the word, and my dead mother
comes lumbering, shaking her rattle
of dry bones.

She walks right on past,
consumed in some task or other
there, in the half remembered.

It's OK. She's gone. I've poured wine.
Perhaps soon, I'll feed this day's
soul hunger with potato soup.

Outside the night
deepens like an arm chair
soft, velvety, and dark.

I suppose the blackbird has found a cosy
and closed her eyes.
I wish it good sleep

and that, like me, it will wake
in the first grey of dawn
and give thanks for its life.

The Butcher's Steel

When I lost my heirlooms
my nephew gave me
his grandfather's honing steel.

In all of the years of its time, this steel
knows my father's hands the best.
His hands, long gone.

I hold it in my hand like my father did
feel the cold of steel, the warmth of wood
a touch of love.

At the table of my childhood
he prepares to carve, slides the knife
down the steel, swish swish swish swish

the rhythm of it in my mind even now
as keen as the blade is keen
as keen as the faces around the table

as keen as the dog's eyes.
It slices through time like the knife
slices the meat

cuts the fibres of the muscle
of some affable animal
with liquid eyes.

Oh yes, it had eyelashes that it batted dumbly.
It had a velvet nose and a heart as red
and as beating as yours.

It was as lively as the creatures
that will consume you
when you are meat.

Each of the keen children around the table
already knows this truth, as my father serves
with carving fork and knife.

Gravy poured, the vegetables are placed
according to the needs of each body
and its red and beating heart.

And now, all this time later,
all of those hearts still beat
except for his.

But here with the butcher's steel
in my hand
is his.

Self-portrait, Adelaide Hills, 21 August 2020

After Peter Bakowski

I am many selves, some of them
want to please all of the people all of the time.
This is impossible, not least because
they have enough trouble pleasing themselves.

And yet the sun shines feebly between clouds.
Backyard trees that I don't know
burst into leaf and flower. Camellias cast
red blossoms on the ground and swell
yet more buds.

Why do those selves in me want to please?
What deep insecurity or fear was born in caves
and trod the hunt and danced with thudding feet
to end up here? What portion
the bowing of heads in churches,
witch hunts, or other battles?

Where is my family with their sweet puddings
and kisses on foreheads before sleep?
Are you my family, all of you strange hordes
of people, living and dying in your own lives
baring your teeth to protect your own?

Please don't take an axe to me
if my poem doesn't please.

Camellias don't laugh at themselves.
They don't do irony. They are much too busy
with all that sap and photosynthesis.
They are completely without fear.

Mending

One uses soft thread
to mend a damaged skin
leather to leather
skin to skin

One sews with stitches
firm and soft enough
to hold together
to mend the rend
to close the wound
to strengthen the weakness
to fortify the vulnerability
to heal.

The mend will show.
You have been in those bad lands
and you have survived
but the mend will show.
So wear your scars visible
a badge of honour.

Look, People. Look, see.
Here are my scars.
These scars describe me.
They describe the country
of my past
but these scars
will not define me.

Changing Colours

In the years before fire stripped me bare,
I was so confident that I used my colours straight.

Red was red or vermillion
occasionally slumping towards maroon.

Yellow was the colour
of a child's crayon-drawing of the sun.

Green was backlit grass in the morning
replete with magpie listening with his feet.

Blue was the sea or sky
or the eyes of my dead son.

Even that
did not strip me bare.

I still had to prove myself or something
make money or fame.

I was still carrying
my mother.

These days I am as pure as a teardrop
and there are many of those.

There are many of those,
washing, washing.

By now my colours are so muted
they hardly know themselves.

Still, dandelions know their true colour,
as does the sky between rain squalls.

There are a million different greens
pushing up through the char.

And red? Can you forget the colour
of fire?

While Weeding and Staking Seedlings

With my hands in the earth
my heart in my hands
my heart in my hands in earth that fed me
for many a year.

My soul would lie down here and sleep.
Surely my great weariness
would seep out into this good earth.
Stars would wheel across the sky
perhaps a late and waning moon.
And in the morning, the sun would rise
and I would turn my face towards it
like a plant. I would rise refreshed
having dreamt the dreamings of the land.

But in the meantime it is enough
to feel its grit between my fingers
to blacken my nails with it.
I pull weeds and stake the seedling trees.
With my hands in earth, attached as they are
to my wounded heart, I listen.
I hear myself apologising for the acts
of human kind. I apologise for being human.

But the earth answers,
'Humans are part of what I am.
Humans have a right to be here.
Humans are part of my whole.
They just need to come back to me.
They need to lie on me and feel their true place:

that they are one small species among many
that the earth owes them nothing and gives everything
that earth is their mother and earth will
receive their bodies when they die
and because of that, they need not hurry
nor worry, nor tangle their thoughts about tomorrow.
They simply need to lie down here and close their eyes.
Let the moon shine and the stars light their nightly piss.
In the morning, the sun will rise
and they will turn to face it like plants
and they will know their place
in the scheme of things.'

Between Earth and Sky

I love this earthen hillside with all
of its individual living things, even
the weeds with their vigour and cheek, even
as I uproot them.

If I have a prayer it is to enliven space, to fill this gap
between earth and sky with living things.

I think it's called gardening, though nature
creates a garden anyway.
Mushrooms and mosses have begun
the long process of making soil from dirt.

Last night, birds came: magpies, parrots.
Somehow I perceived more, as if there were many others
that did not show themselves or voice their presence.

There are many angry spirits roaming the ghost lands
where, just now, above the burnt earth, space replaces life.

There are many sad spirits also.
I am one of them.
And guilty.
Me too.

How came it that humans are more enamoured
of metal and cyberspace than of this earthworm?
We are so busy looking into the abyss of our phones
that we forget we will feed these worms soon enough.

We are so blinkered by light that we don't see
that our young may fall before they breed.
The earth could easily take us.
The earth could take us while we tap buttons.

These weeds in my hands let fall seed.
If my favoured plants do not thrive
they certainly will.

They know their purpose. They rush
to fill the space between earth
and sky.

Pandora's Box is leaky

Hope springs eternal, they say
but my facebook feed tells a different story.
How about you? What do you think will happen
next week, next year? What will be the outcome
of the latest political puppeteering?
What future the earth, baking in human greed?
What will we be doing in 2040?
And what are we doing about it?
Well, I'm looking at my facebook feed. You?

But what if we all decide right now
that we have, in fact, got enough?
What if the greediest people on the planet
decide that too?
What if we give to the needy, not just a fish
or a fishing rod, but a place in our hearts?
What if we love unconditionally?
What if we knew we were loved unconditionally?
What if?

My words flow out of a plastic pen
bought from a plastic shop
onto paper from a dead tree.
And death is fine as a form of protein
for our words, or the life of another.
It's not morbid to say it will take me.
But in the meantime, how shall I live?

I want to focus on what I want. How else would I get it?
And what I want is a good outcome to all of this.
I want us humans to love each other enough
to protect the source of life
to protect this vibrant being: Earth
and to live in harmony.
I hope Earth's blood sacrifices begin
with the greediest but I'll willingly
give my life for its survival.
And it will survive,
with or without humans,
it will survive.

also

as if there was
nothing more to do
I sit under the plum tree
and petals also
fall on me

Tanka sequence, September 2020

having been
burnt to its roots
the parsley thrives
and I take it
as a metaphor

the wagtail
on its wings of frailty
expresses
in its flight
something like joy

the heart
that breaks and breaks and breaks
until
there's beauty
even in that

a seedling weed
its virility pushing
towards seed
what will I plant now
in the burnt garden of my soul

these happy flowers
of the onion weed
nod their heads
and here I am with
my murderous intent

twittering
out of sight
some unknown bird
about its business
of eating and loving

following
the heart's happiness
I find
I quite enjoy
hanging out washing

that I am earth
lying here on it
gazing at the sky
sometimes the mind
needs rest, and so…

Gifts

Hey, Little Blue Bird,
I'm weeding your home
and planting a place
for you to nest.

A friend gave me these spiny wattles.
She gave tomato relish, kitchen knives,
and milkweed seeds. Apparently
butterflies lay eggs on milkweed.

Pickles and prickles, and a nursery for butterflies,
since our life burnt down, we have received
so many gifts. I hold my heart and I prostrate
before the generosity of humanity.

It's good that I know no avaricious politicians
or the thief who stole our fire pump.
I feel sad for the greedy people.
How damaged must they be, to be so needy?

No one I know. Our people opened
their hearts and wallets and wardrobes
and showered us with love.
Even total strangers showered us with love.

They opened their hearts, as people do when
witnessing trauma but, Little Bird, the world
is full of traumas, one upon the other.
We are tired and curl up under the covers.

Hurt hearts must rest. I wish them good sleep.
I wish them visionary dreams of a healthy world.
I wish them daytime awareness
of health and love and of interconnection

with you, among others, Little Blue Bird.
Meanwhile I plant a nesting spot for you
and milkweed for butterflies,
and butterflies for magpies and their kin.

The magpies warble in the blackened skeletons of trees.
Here, in the soft black earth are kangaroo tracks
and you hop about with your wives
amidst the luscious and vibrant growth of weeds.

Meditations after Loss

Still I miss this or that.
I miss the little grey house that nestled
into the hillside as if it belonged.

I miss the trees, their shade, their presence.
I miss the life that fed on them.

Surely life will come back to the earth,
at first not diverse, and never, perhaps,
what it was, but life will come back to the earth.

Soon I will live in a shiny new house
that looks as if it could fly. A crow perhaps
or a hawk lifting off the ground
slowly and awkwardly as heavy birds do.

I miss the yellow-tailed black cockatoos
that came this time of year for pine cones
and stayed for the hakeas.

The hakea stumps have eleven leaves
on each shoot.
                Soon, my cockies, soon…

The bones of the pine trees stand
black and shiny
waiting for the chainsaw.

I do not want to tread this path of loss again
and neither do you, you, there, reading this
with your empathy and dread.
What lesson will you take from my words?

Take this: the reason you voyeur my pain
and the reason I show it to you is because
we are relations, you and I,
my brother, my sister

and we are related
to the tiniest fly and the greatest tree.
They have no words
and so I give them words.

They say, We are relations, you and I,
my brother, my sister, we are
we are.

tired as a wet rag

tired as a wet rag
I'm sick of it all
twenty twenty

Paper Stars

On 24 August, our builder, Alex, sent us a photo of a digger rearranging the earth on our house site. It had begun! He always said that he would get us in by Christmas, but the weather was wet, wet, wet. All the nay-sayers and anyone who knew anything about anything said it was impossible, especially since between the concrete being laid and the roof being on it was wet, wet, wet.

In the third week of November, the South Australian government put the state into lockdown again. It was designed to stop an outbreak of Covid and was to be for a week. Alex rang me, saying, 'I'm so sorry but we won't get you in by Christmas.' I answered, 'Oh well, It's just a date. Don't worry. But miracles do happen.' Two days later the lockdown was lifted because it was based on false information. Alex rang. 'You've got your Christmas miracle,' he said.

On 23 December, he handed us the keys.

first gift
for a new house
paper stars

Bob and the Crows

land still black –
the eager eye
of a shrike thrush

In the lounge room, on the armchair next to him, is a shrike thrush. It has found its way through a maze of rooms with open doors, to sit beside him. The little bird goes out the way he came in, as if he knows this house better than us, and he probably does.

It is a year since the fire took the district, a year since he came into our old house and sat on the top of the door and piped his shrill note, requesting meat. This little bird is the same Bob, who we knew before. He escaped! And he came home! And as soon as we were home, he came to greet us.

And he brought Mrs Bob and Baby Bob! We were so pleased that they could breed when there was so little habitat.

The birdscape has changed around here. Where once we had families of magpies, now we have crows with their gloss and their raspy voices. There are magpies close by but they don't come to the house.

My main activity for this second year is planting for habitat, insects and nectar. Other birds come back slowly.

black skeleton trees
– the celebratory voices
of crows

New House 1

The hollowness of a cave, our voices resound in all of its corners. This summer sunlight streams in, as blinding as the darkness of mind, catacombs remembered, all the lost libraries and bones, skulls as clean as this new house where we tread with our charcoaled feet, ground memories, things you can't place or find. Never mind. We bring the stuff of a life: cushions, slippers, doonas, the hard-backed chairs, wooden spoons. What to do now? How to think? How to clear the charcoal from the mind? Hang pictures, place trinkets, bury self in days of solitaire, wait for the cloud in the fish tank to settle. There is no fish tank, that's a metaphor, but there is a lot of dust. The topsoil is loose, windborne. That is true, but it's also a metaphor.

Come now, heart of mine, settle down here, you have been walking through miles and miles of charcoal and bones in glaring sunshine. But now you are home. Now you can draw blinds, close eyes, rest your head on feathers. Sleep. Dream. Wake.

Here, another game of solitaire?

New house 2

I don't want to whinge, because everything is hunky-dory. It is. Couldn't be better. Probably, this agitation is a habit of mind and will pass. But I don't want you to think that when it's over, it's over. There is still cutlery to put away, and other trinkets, and the mind is a vast cupboard. Where did I put the chopping boards and how did I end up with so many saucepans, none of which work? But look, here comes another saviour bearing pots that do. Thank the living for saviours. I plan to become one soon. What else is life for?

Come, saviour, my friend, my loved one. Have coffee more delicious than ever before from this new machine. Sit down here on this new old chair. Help us fill the beautiful corners of this building with what it is that makes a home. Laughter is good, but if it's too early for that, then love will suffice.

New house 3

At home in a house made of some unknown material that you could take a blowtorch to, I mourn a little that I can no longer say, 'my little wooden house', but never mind, what's gone is gone. My dead stand behind me with their hands on my shoulders. They instruct me to loosen the muscles in my neck, to lean towards the sunshine like it's a friend, to take what's now and make poetry of it. Poetry, according to my dead, is life in black letters, and they crave it. Even the dead have desires, they tell me, and instruct me to live as if I would die next minute: that alert, that open, that excited. They say it is lovely that I once had a little wooden house. They say, tell us one thing that is not made of earth, and instruct me to take the house that is made of unknown materials and live in it as if I would die next minute: that alert, that open, that excited.

Walking Through Walls

This new house is a skeleton on another skeleton.
It's as if the old house still exists in this space.
I walk through its walls. I stand
in the bedroom beside the old bed.
If I close my eyes, I can look out of the old window
at the vibrant plum tree and into the eyes of cattle
that have since become meat.

It's odd.
The memories dissolve into reality:
the cool concrete underfoot
the quietness of double glazing and fine joinery.
The wind flutes across the chimney
louder and longer than the old one.
It's a sad sound, like mourning.
Well, of course there is mourning.
That prior life is just below the surface of now,
all the lost things, the sunlight
on the bathroom wall, for example.

But, let's face it,
it was trouble, that old building,
with its moving joints and broken things.
This new one is attaining soul
slowly but surely.
One makes a home by sleeping there.
And the presence of the old building,
its warmth, and the love in its crevasses,
are still there, just out of sight
though sometimes, I walk through its walls.

Some darkness broke your heart

but do not give darkness to darkness.
Do not cover that wound.
Do not build a shield around it like
an old woman hunched over her grief.

A wound heals from the inside, fleshes healthy.
Allow crows to clean the fester,
transmute your pain to flight.
Allow the sunshine in: light, light, light, light.

Sometime later, you will hear yourself laugh.
Your grief will be a shining medal on your chest,
reflective but inert,
and you will know healing.

Last Red

The last red still touches the top of the hill opposite.
The sky beyond is pale, summer's fulsome blue
faded to lemon, as the bruise of twilight
climbs from the east.

Today a pair of wedge-tail eagles
lifted over the paddock next door,
close enough to see their eyes.
They glided to my favourite picture tree.

That tree, recently burnt, wears its nudity
like an old woman, my mother perhaps,
looking like the transition she was in,
her bones a structure to hang soft crepe skin upon.

The tree, no longer sapping, still hosts a myriad of life.
Who knows what death is, after a lifetime of stages?
The red has gone from the hill.
Now it wears its silver grass like eveningwear.

After the Great Undoing

After the great undoing:
time spent in timelessness,
the body doing its body things,
the mind away on business,
the heart a bruised petal from a rose
that bloomed only days
after fire had burnt it brittle.
The will to life, so strong, so strong.

I don't know what I've been since then
or what I've done
but now I have a roof and walls.
There are windows that open and shut.
My body has a place to belong
but the wind howls across the treeless places
and whatever I was before, I'm not.

The shamans speak of this.
The initiate is torn asunder
and remade from bits of feather and bone
tatters found amid charcoal and ashes
blood of earth, hair of grass.
'Before' is made of memories pasted
into a story that changes with the telling.
Useless, really.

So you bring the one who always
wanted to be you and you make it you.
And then you begin the work
of 'after'.

This New House After Fire

This new house that I'm living in
is beautiful like a song of joy in clear morning air,
as clean as that, as pure.

I learn to love it as one loves
in an arranged marriage between good people.
I talk to it. 'Hi, House,' I say, and ask it
to care for us and promise to care for it.
I sing into its echoing corners,
promise laughter and love.
I begin the work of that.
I bring objects: stones and shells, feathers and plants.
I place them, like offerings, on the altar that it is.
It begins to feel warm, heart warm,
and cool on hot days,
as welcoming as a shelter
which, of course, it is.

One day soon, I know,
I will open the silent front door,
heavy, and gliding on its hinges,
and instead of saying, 'Hi, House,'
I'll say, 'Hello, Home.'

There are Times When it is Worth Standing at the Backdoor Looking like a Madwoman and Drumming at the Sky

If, when you see the eagle pair
making their way across the sky
with the rudder of their wedge-shaped tails
angling slightly according to the updraft,
and you take your drum outside and beat it for them,
and if you climb the rise to better see
them circling away and keep drumming,
they will know it is for them and will come circling back
and hang in the air as still as the rabbits who watch them.
They will listen for a while as the drum
sings the heartbeat of Other, and then
they will loft away in the circles of their life,
with not so much the slightest beat of their wings,
and your heart will be big enough to fill the sky
and the drum will speak for a while to it,
and to the sky, and to the sacred earth underfoot.

Near Life

You were a very sick girl, said the surgeon after
I nearly died. I was seventeen and in boisterous health.
I had been writing wills for six months as if I knew,
but I didn't die of a burst appendix.
Even so, part of me did – my childhood perhaps?
I was a different person afterwards.
Shall I list the ways? No. Enough to say that
when I see a native water rat in the twilight,
swimming and drawing his lines of wake
behind him like an arrow before darting into
some hole in mud, there is some symbology to be found,
some parallel to life in general, and my life in particular.

Perhaps they gave me too much morphine or perhaps
that ascent back into life gave me this strange sense
of everything reflecting everything else.
The rat's small body of will is intent on life,
on finding and eating, finding and mating,
while the wake traces each moment for a brief while
before the water stills, and everything is forgotten.
And I think of my life and of those who I have lost,
and I know we all move through life with
our wills propelling our busy limbs and the world
mends after us, like sky being mended
on the surface of black water at dusk.

Brain Tree

In my brain is a tree.
Its trunk is the brain stem,
its leaves are thoughts, a myriad of them,
many that look the same.
Its roots spread out along the byways
to the very edges of me where they take in
air and sunshine and sustenance.
The trunk divides in two, one leader
in each half of my brain, and in each,
amid the complications of branches is a crow.

They sing.

Now, you may not recognise the voice of a crow
as song because they've had a bad rap,
but they sing of sunshine and wings, grubs,
the dank delicious flesh of the freshly dead,
and they sing of love and babies, just like we all do.

And what they sing with, is air, like the air
on the intricate surface of our skin
or in each alveoli of our lungs,
the air that courses through
all of those byways of brain and body,
and trunk and leaves.

No wonder they sing. Don't you?

Fifteen Months After Wildfire

(after 'The Peace of Wild Things' by Wendell Berry)

Sometimes, when I despair at this view,
this beautiful, wide view that once
was the intimate domesticity of trees,
I go and lie down under
the blackened corpses of giants,
amongst the groundcovers and mosses,
the lilies and the weeds, and I feel
their thrum of life, their steady growth, their
complete lack of judgement or grief, and I think
that I too could be as simple as that, and I too
could just get on with growing.

Learning to Love Yet Another Thing That I Didn't Love Before

Oh, my earth – true earth of home –
you invite all and sundry to lie on you
and sprout.

There are so many weeds
in the burnt lands that I'm learning
to love them and their myriad forms,
their fleshing leaves and brilliant flowers.

For instance, I'm learning to love the vivacity
of thistledown, flying, or nestling in piles inches deep,
all those billion billion seeds,
ready and ready and ready.

The rains will come and then we'll see
the result of work not done, and wind,
and the joy of sprouting.

Oh, my earth, you love dandelions, the tenacity
of their roots delving, drawing your potential skyward,
transforming it into green bodies that play with wind
like a child's joy dancing, life of life of life of life.

Oh, my earth – true earth of home –
how can I love you and not love
this dandelion with its sunshine face.

Saying Goodbye

On the day of the fires, after we drove out,
I went back for his walking sticks and
I stood in the lounge room and said Goodbye.

How come part of me knew
that I'd never stand there again
when so much of me didn't?

In any case I walked out the door
with nothing
but those two wooden sticks.

I walked out the door
with its scratches from cats,
its coat hooks, and imbedded grease

where my children's hands had trailed
their sticky sweetness and sometimes
slammed its satisfying weight

where I had greeted loved ones
and friends and the morning air.

I had forgotten until now that, that day,
I said goodbye but it seems to me
I'm still saying goodbye.

Insurance Home Contents Claim

What was in my house that burnt?
Two thousand books, seventeen chairs,
a four-hundred-year-old green Hungarian vase,
the drawings from my grandchildren
and their parents,
photos, love, music, space, tears,
grief and happiness, saucepans,
a fridge full of food,
a plaster cast of one child's face,
a gift of heart from another,
naughtiness written on a door by the third,
the last breath of their childhood and of my youth,
a twenty-year-old Hoya that flowered and dripped nectar,
ants, the sugar spoon from my childhood,
various plastic dinosaurs,
this thing, that thing,
bits of my mother, bits of my father.

We took our winter coats and computers,
cameras, citizenship papers, odd documents,
a couple of his walking sticks, and a few clothes.
It's sixteen months later and I'm making lists.
Already my new knickers are grey.

In No Time

This cold morning, we rise
blunder from toilet to coffee, stretch
and yawn the air's rising light

Soon cars will wind up the valley throwing
beams of light around the mist
My candle will sputter and go out

On the ridge, magpies flute
notes of round sound
that tumble over the landscape

Sweet people, my family
and ones bent on gain, let me tell you: this
is all there is

It appears to be hard or easy
It appears to be this or that
We feel happy or not

But all differences are
of one great whole wherein we abide
at once one, at once two

Sweet people, my family
and ones bent on gain, let me tell you: this
is all there is

The air is still like a lung waiting
witness of sky and autumn
The earth opens its pores to moisture

You and I will rest there soon enough
in the vibrant eternity of no time
wherein we already are

The Space Between

After reading Wendell Berry

Oh, Wendell, I love how you leave your troubles at your door
and step outside where the sky is hugely full of nothing and
every creature lives its life in the only way it knows.

Today, outside the bedroom window, a crow alighted
on a charcoaled stump. In the sunlight, the wet stump
was as black and glossy as he, and just as carefree.

The difference was animation, though goodness knows what
is going on in the stump. I am not a beetle or an ant
or a subatomic particle, so I wouldn't know.

I don't know what is going on in the crow either
but its eye was at once eager and calm. Of course, it looked like
it belonged in a pulpit where it could discourse on death

and resurrection since it knows about such things.
Meantime, it stopped the grind of my mind
for a moment and stepped into the space between.

Gratitude

The sunshine on my feet
The trees and their vigour
Fungi doing their work amongst roots
Food: the everyday potato, parsley
peppers and tomatoes, thyme
The love of friends and family
That they accept my love
Starshine: that immensitude
Storms: storms of the heart and
storms of the sky
Water falling from clouds, fresh cold
Water in a glass
Wind that whips my face with my hair
Generosity
Things given in times of need
Plenitude plenitude
I accept I accept I accept
Humility

Chimney Blues

When the wind plays flute
with the chimney
it sounds mournful

like keening. In this country
of charcoal and crows
it sounds appropriate.

But the rain
beats its percussion onto soil
and things grow.

I hear a bird that I don't recognise and I rejoice.
Another bird is here in the burnt lands!
Slowly things grow and animals come back.

Our human hearts grow new flesh
over old wounds and
we stop picking at the scabs.

But everyone loves a sad song
and Blues are the only tunes
the chimney knows.

Not the Time for Making

In this new house of solid sand
it's not the time for making.
Making is done and dusted, burnt and gone.

Now is the time for mending
gathering all the little shards
and gluing them together.

Perhaps the bindings will be gold,
a precious metal, desirable and malleable,
but more likely, everyday glue
or double-sided sticky tape.

These thoughts are disparate.
They are messy like the fragments
of a former life, shattered and scattered.

Did you know that when crystals:
amethyst, carnelian, quartz:
go through fire, they shatter?

It's all so much sand actually, but sharp.
It will take some time for the world
to wear them smooth, and that's why
this is not the time for making.

This is the time for mending.

Awake in the night thinking

Awake in the night thinking
of all the things I have to worry about
and all the things I have to be thankful for
and you came up

you with your beautiful heart.
Thank you for the generosity therein.
I want to say that the human race
is composed of hearts like yours.
Mostly.

Sure, there's greed but greed
is just a sad sickness not a blight.
The only need that distorts
is the need for love
and thankfully that's free
and plentiful.
Mostly.

A Gift of Oxygen

(For Jo)

The fine yellow potential
The sapling and the burnt soil
The friend bearing a gift tree
Love that seeps into the soil around here

Nature that just keeps on growing
always growing and changing
sprouting and dying and sprouting

This green shield we have around the world
How plants seek to grow into any space
into every space: each small crack in the sidewalk,
each area that is exposed to sky

How we live under their canopy
in the thin space between arbour and earth
and are only now learning that
we have no choice but to seek their protection

And here comes my friend, bearing in her arms
– arms that enfold the ones she loves –
a sapling of a ginkgo tree
its fine yellow potential

its gift of oxygen

Dear Friend

I'm sorry that you still limp
down the corridors of pain.
I turned back and held out my hand
but it turns out we were
in different worlds by then:

you, in a bureaucratic nightmare
with mud on your shoes,
me, weeding on a hillside in a sun shower
getting wet, amid daisies.

What can I do? I bend my ear
to the daisies and they tell me
this is the time of my healing.
The earth works constantly
on becoming fertile, and I must
look forward, not back.

But, my friend, your nightmare of pain
will end, it can't not if you keep walking
one step, at a time.
Therefore keep hope, keep hope.

I'm waiting for you on this hillside
amid daisies.

(Where others in the community had survivors' guilt from the
very beginning, those of us who moved into our houses earlier
than others went through it, because we understood that others
behind us were still struggling day to day, with decisions, bu-

reaucrats, and other problems, including friends and family who couldn't understand why they were still fragile and traumatised.)

Planting Microseris Lanceolata

It's almost dark,
twilight of a full moon
as I tuck the little woman
into the clay, where she may
reach down with her supple feet
and, come autumn, grow thighs worthy
of a middle-aged woman.
In a few years perhaps
I'll cook her fat legs and put fat on mine.

But in the meantime,
welcome, Yam Daisy,
to this land where fire raged.
I plant you where I pull out dandelions.
You can do the job they did,
pull the goodness of the deep earth
up into air, breathe leaves, smile flowers.
May your thistledown float on the best wind.
May your kin prosper in this
bushland confusion
of sapling trees and fire fungi.

We are kin, you and I,
my heart is already in the earth,
my legs, ankle deep.

Owning Sorrow

Sorrow turns to anger
anger to rage
rage to destruction
or to burning oneself out
from the inside.

Or sorrow turns to pain.
Either way one drags
one's sorrow behind one
like a dead dog on a leash.

But the sorrow held
by our Aboriginal people
our original inhabitants
our First Nations folk
our knowledge keepers
is of another order.

This sorrow is of the earth and
if we white people do not
pick up their dead dog and carry it
it will bury us.

Stories

Back before we lost our stories, the sun
made its way across the sky as the god it
surely is and on setting, made love
with the earth all night long ('union'
as it was called in those days)
and when he rose again in the morning
flowers turned towards him like
hair cells of the earth aroused by desire.

Even now their yearning for the morning sun
reminds us of the earth's love, though now
our stories are called knowledge and tell us
that the sun is separate like some great ego
that the earth spins around.

Our stories separate this from that and put
each into its own rationalist box.
We make boxes even for our own selves,
separate from the earth, the sun,
the flower and each other.

Two things: it's lonely here in my box
and secondly: since the sun and earth
no longer make love, the sun's ego
has become so strong that flowers
turn their faces away.

They turn to face the earth like jilted lovers.
Wilting, it's called.

Caterpillar in a Paper Daisy

Look. Here is the fragile body of a green caterpillar
curled in the soft centre of a paper daisy.
All those spiky petals, and here it is.
My heart lifts at this short story like it does
for the open mind of the child, here, gazing also.

Oh, sweet child, the prickles of the petals of the paper daisy
were a sharp road for this small creature, but now
it is in its soft bed, sleeping.
The sky is its blue room, the good earth its foundations
as the good earth is the foundation
of your life and of mine.

The caterpillar opens its jaws and eats the days of its life
until something calls (perhaps it is the lengthening nights?)
and then it spins for itself a castle from the matter
of its own body, a small chamber wherein
it will dream itself into a new form
or the new form will dream a caterpillar's changes,
and the moist structure of will-be wings.

Oh, child, I take you in my arms, wrap my heart around you
and hold you through these precious moments of your childhood,
wherein you develop the soft and crumpled form of wings.
When the time comes I will allow myself to be discarded
while you puff them into strong and beautiful structures
that will carry you into your adult life.

And, though I will know little of it, I will see you
flitting here and there in the serious business of your life
until, perhaps, you will lead me to the whorl of a cradle
to gaze upon the soft body of an infant
like the green curl of a caterpillar in a paper daisy.

Imagine Living on Nectar

(Part of a longer poem written for *Flocking Together*, a bushfire recovery and arts project produced by illuminart Australia and Fabrik Arts + Heritage)

It begins and ends with the earth
with soil and the sun
and plants converting sunshine to sugar

All the myriad animals eating thereof
and animals eating other animals thereof
and the rich soil that lives
on the spent life of others
this worm, that beetle.

Here comes Blue Wren with his wives, flitting and chatting,
working over this fallen log, that patch of earth.
There is plenty to go around on the level of bugs.

There is plenty to go around even for mankind
if they care
if they learn again to care for
everything
of which they're part.

The parrot, the tiny fly,
the worm and the giant tree
all of the animals and plants that live
in this world of plenty.

In this tree hollow, parrots.
In that, swallows.
In that messy pile of sticks, the baby magpies
open their mouths like orchids.

The magpie mum comes and stuffs a worm into the squawking.
Big sister comes and stuffs a worm into the squawking.
Dad comes and stuffs a worm into the squawking.

On the nest edge
facing into the wind
the baby magpie tests air
each wing feather trembling.

Its first flight is more down than up.
A human happens by and lifts him
from ground to a low branch.

The human thinks it's the only animal
with empathy but that's not true, even though
each animal loves its life.

The thornbills come through the bushland
cleaning the leaves as they come
like love.

Like love, honeyeaters
dip furred tongues
into the throats of flowers.

Imagine living on nectar!
Pollen dusts their faces.
Their faces marry pollen to this next flower.

Seeds form, they fall
they settle into the earth where
they wait in their own time
seed time

and one day vibrate their potential
into a first exploring root
into cotyledon leaves.

What happens in between the pollen on his face
and the tiny sprout?

There's breaking and dying.
There's being consumed.
There's being transformed.

There's good weather and there's bad.
There's floods and frost
and storms with wind and hail.
There's fire and destruction.

The destruction hurts the hearts
of every creature
and all the plants but such
is the wheel of life
that shoots sprout.

Rain falls on damaged earth.
Moss and lichen begin their work.
Fungi makes networks beneath the earth.

They say fungi even feeds dead trees so that
they often stand long after they should have fallen.

The human heart is like that.
It gets up, it falls, it gets up, it gets up, it gets up.

It puts out new green feelers.
Finds joy in the first shoots, the first flowers
just like the myriad creatures.

You want an image of tenacity?
A butterfly comes to the burnt world just as surely
as if nothing had happened.
It flits from daisy to daisy.

The daisies delve roots deep into soil
and make flowers.
They drop their dead stalks and leaves
onto earth, making soil.

A seed stimulated by fire
or by frost or the flooded earth
begins to vibrate
begins to tremble with the stirring of potential.

What will it be? A wattle, a banksia,
a kennedia cloaking black earth with red flowers?

All the shooting plants.
Legumes feeding the earth.
The earth cures itself.

And look!
Here comes blue wren with only one wife
but it begins.

A season or three
and there will be a family twittering their gossip
twittering their gossip
and working over the earth.

Here are moss and lichen.
There, grasses flowering and shedding pollen.
There's sneezing.
Here, the scent of boronia.
Here a banksia with seed pods like gremlins
that open only after fire.
There casuarinas shushing air.

There are clouds and rain.
There's water in the air
and listen, listen.
There's birdsong

So many songs no one can know them all.
Even the birds don't know them all.

A butcher bird composes new music each day
and the baby magpie already knows its songs.

The fledgling parrot squawks its feed-me squawk
and mum regurgitates insects and half-digested seed.
Each to their own.

Listen, can you hear the bronze wing pigeon making
its sound, a sound as soft as a petal?

Are you sick?
Are you sad of heart?
We are all sad of heart but here
is a green leaf
a soft bed of moss
of grass.

Are you sad of heart?
Here is a flower to gladden it.
Here chocolate lilies scent the air
giving, giving.

Listen
birdsong is sung
indiscriminately into air.

That song is for you also.

Perhaps you have been taught that it's all selfish genes
but you can have that bird song
and you can keep it.
You can let it gladden your heart.

And when your heart delights, you can also sing.
The world will be glad of it.

Perhaps each of us sings the world into being
just like the first bird sang the world into being.

You of glad heart, perhaps yours may be the heart
that gladdens other hearts
that cures greed.

Think of that
could song cure greed?

Well, let's start with grief and move on to greed

Before long we will sing the world into a new dawn.
We come together in our hearts and sing
even from our own trees.

We have everything in our hearts:
this dawn, that sunset, the vibrant earth, the glad insect.
We sing to the world, to this beautiful world
that we save with our love every day.

Every morning
bees awaken
and begin work
in the bounty of flowers.

Beetles turn the great tree
into humus
into soil
into earth.

Mushrooms sprout otherworldly heads
while underground
they continue their great act
of healing.

Connections, connections,
do you feel it yet?

You, with your human heart
at once mushroom, at once ant,
the very air you breathe
is the outbreath of plants,
plants with their roots deep in your love,
the love of earth.

It begins and ends with the earth
with soil and the sun
and plants converting sunshine to sugar.

Hiraeth n. (Welsh)

The first paragraph is from a meme that begins, 'Hiraeth n. (Welsh)'

'Nostalgia for ancient places to which we cannot return.
It is the echo of the lost places of our soul's past and
our grief for them. It is in the wind, and the rocks, and the waves.
It is nowhere and it is everywhere.'

It is my heart in the skeleton branches of beloved trees.
It is the air space of the place where others stood.
It is the wood I set in the grate with its memories of shining.
It is the wall of the lost house that
I walk through while entering the bedroom.
It is my hands in earth blackened by char.
It is the small wound that
bleeds onto the soil, red tears of longing.
It is the blood that does not know what it is
but misses something dreadfully.

Who knows what we were?
People like me have 'before' and 'after'
and don't remember that, before,
we felt a crooked sense of loss for that which
may never have been.

Sitting in the dusk watching the light go down,
the heart's taut strings attach to every loss
even those that are not mine.
Darkness is a blessing, groping the way by touch from this
to this, a relief from the searing light
on every invoice and obligation.

In the fields, the grasses nod heads that
fill with the weight of next year's seed.
They nod in the early mist and surely give thanks.
Or not. Each moment is another moment of sap.
The black soil is fertile with loss.
My life is fertile with loss.
My loss is in the wind, and the rocks,
and the waves of grass like water on the hillside.
It is in photographs that no longer sit on the sill
It is a sill that isn't.
It is a loved cup that has returned to the earth.
It is nowhere and everywhere.
It is in the black earth growing potatoes,
potatoes that I give to my loved ones.

We eat of our loss and endeavour
to open our hearts to the taste of potato,
to be in the moment of potato,
like the grass is in the moment of wind.

Two years and thirteen days afterwards

Sometimes I wonder why the time of recovery was so difficult, why I ended up with a type of spastic tic in my throat, why the stomach pain, why the ongoing symptoms of anxiety. One of the many blessed things about the brain is that you forget. But does the subconscious? How do you settle it?

The following was written after an interaction with a friend who I hadn't met for a year. I assume I was being a bit one-dimensional in my conversation, because she said something like, 'I guess there is quite a lot to it.' It made me realise that most people had forgotten all about it, something other victims complain about, because their families and friends think they are weak or overreacting. Many of those people have still not got foundations laid for their new homes. Two years on and they are still struggling with bureaucrats. So I wrote this but I still need to ask the question about the subconscious.

There's not much to fire recovery...

apart from getting the basics of knickers and notebooks, tooth-brushes and medications; apart from the paperwork of proving you exist; apart from researching how to, and applying for, all of those documents; apart from making all the decisions about what sort of house you want (while you are still in a state of complete shock); apart from filling forms to get grants; organising people to help clean up; doing the clean-up; making sure it is safe for the people working on the clean-up; organising the insurance; coping with the loss; worrying if you'll have enough money; researching and learning about what a BAL (Bushfire Attack Level) rating is; interacting with the CFS to find out what your BAL rating actually is, what that means in terms of the building, and what other things the CFS require so that the building is defendable; apart from interacting with the council to work out if they will let you use your septic system any more; apart from needing to find out if there's asbestos in the waste or not, and what that means; apart from learning how to handle the burnt land, to control weeds, and facilitate regrowth; apart from finding time to do that work; apart from doing that work and finding a place to pee on the hill that used to be nooks but was burnt to completely visible space; apart from having no water or roof to collect water to even take a sip while you are working in the heat in masks and gloves; apart from rummaging through the waste to see if there is anything of value (sentimental or otherwise) left at all; apart from trying to find out if your concrete tank still holds water, and researching how to fix said tank that doesn't hold water and how to set up pipes and pumps and tanks for the water infrastructure again; apart from discussing and handling the disagreements with neighbours about what sort of fences you need and who will pay for them; apart from trying to work out how to keep the earth on the hill when the rains come; apart from all the decisions about the aesthetics of the building you're going to live in for so many years, what the colour of the roof should be, for example, and finding out from the authorities that the colour choices for the building are grey, grey, or ugly green (unless you want to hold up building for months while you apply to use a different colour); apart from working out how to get the fallen timber into piles for burning, or piles for firewood; how and when (between too wet and fire season) to safely burn the three piles (as big as buses) of broken trees; apart from choosing, paying for, organising delivery of, and making sure the timing is right for the white goods, bathroom fixtures, tiles, and cabinetry.

And this is not to mention the individual decisions about the building, the civil works, earthworks, stabilisation of banks of turned earth, and the to-ing and fro-ing with the council and engineers and the CFS and other government agencies, much of which was done for us by our daughter, who project-managed the building, designed, and did most of the architecture, even though she was not yet an architect. She also held my hand through the decision-making process of the colour choices for the interior of the house (which ended up grey, grey, and white).

And, once back on the land (feeling blessed because we are so lucky to have an almost-architect for a daughter and a builder who is also a friend), apart from learning to live in a house that you feel no love for at first, that feels strange like something that belongs to a real estate advertisement; how to manage the regrowth, and build a garden that is fire retardant and hopefully beautiful, fertile, and productive for us and the many natural creatures who lived here, and hopefully will live here again; continued research and decisions about what is a weed and what isn't; apart from organising wonderful volunteers to help plant more than 700 plants that were gifted by so many green thumbs; apart from decisions and the installation of more water infrastructure to water the plants.

Apart from learning how to receive help. Apart from the exhaustion.

Apart from all of the above, and much that I have already forgotten, or have not written, there was nothing to do these past two years, but worry, like the rest of the population, about Covid and the state of the planet.

Dandelion Lessons

The wind does what wind does; it blows.
The dandelion flowers nod, they succumb
to the forces acting upon them.
They become more strong, simply feeding
the bending stalks, and allowing movement.
Flexibility, it's called. There's a lesson there.

Meanwhile they do not stop for a moment
this vital interaction with sunshine
receiving it, transforming it,
carrying its power into the soil where their roots
seek out moist places and minerals
and interact with mycelium that
interacts with other forms of life down there
in a massive interconnecting web
like a brain and just as amazing.

But unlike a brain they don't make stories
about how this soil is fertile or not fertile
or the wind rough or gentle.
They just go on with the process
of breathing life and nodding
the bright sunshine faces of their fruiting bodies.
And the wind keeps on blowing
Sometimes blustery, sometimes soft.

A Garden Begins with Violence

A garden begins with violence:
fire or the hoe, a cleaning out,
a smothering, a clean break from the past.

But after the violence, intimacy:
hands that spread seed, tiny packages of hope,
or that cradle a root ball as gently
as a parent washes the head of a newborn,
tucking the roots into the soil and crooning.

Most days, lately, I work over the brassicas
(cabbage and broccoli) wiping off the eggs
of the cabbage white butterfly or squishing
the caterpillars with my loving hands.

Violence and love. Yesterday I found
the empty chrysalis of a parasitic wasp.
They are flitting through the garden right now,
drinking nectar and laying eggs
into the bodies of caterpillars.

They will feed from those bodies until they cut their way out
and settle to spin their own chrysalises.
Meanwhile the caterpillar is so changed by tending them
that it spins extra protection and guards them until it dies.

Today I watched the mating dance
of two cabbage whites.
She settled on a leaf and spread her wings flat,
her black dots like a beacon, while he flittered and fussed.

She will lay eggs of a dubious fate.
The butterflies are plentiful, the caterpillars are plentiful,
the wasps are plentiful, the host plants are plentiful.
Everywhere violence, everywhere love.

Not Woe

Tonight I sat on a stump under the black trees
with their strong trunks reaching up into the night sky
and their filigree of dead twigs.

Of course, the stars came down and sat in their branches
and the moon, lowering to the west, sang a fine clear song
of beauty. Or she would have if I could listen better.

As it was my rattle brain rattled on and on, as it does.
It even spoke a poem to the darkness and only stopped
when it began to speak of woe.

What does the night want to know of woe?
Meanwhile the plants were resting in the earth
breathing out their in-breaths of tomorrow.

Down the hill kangaroos were grazing
and frogs sang from the creek.
The stars glittered their supreme indifference

and those fire scarred trees stood blacker than darkness,
like yogis with their palms up.
I had sadness and I let it go.

There is no use for sadness any more, said the trees. Now we are
to stand here being beautiful, an illustration of tenacity and firmness
while life pushes up from the earth into new growth.

Nothing to do now, but get on with it.

Out the Other Side

Who knows why some people
get eaten by their trauma, some fight, and some
wait beneath it and come out the other side
full of light and love and joy.

Here, People, is a little pill for that: what if this
is your only life? And what if this moment
is the only one you'll ever have?
And now this moment and this.

Life is made up of them, we know it,
but they are slippery characters it seems.
Or perhaps our minds are the slippery characters
consumed, as they are, by doubt and fear.

I'm good at lecturing but all my moments drift by
while I worry about something. Or regret something else.

I want joy.
It's a deceptively simple word, three letters,
and beautiful, like a flower, a daisy.

Would it be possible to stand like a flower,
simply, breathing it in, or to find it
tickling your toes like grass, or to feel it
in your belly like sherbet on the tongue?

Can I call it to me like a wild bird?
What seed should I offer so that it will
fly in here and spread its wings in my chest.

In the east, on the dark edge of night
are three orange stripes of cloud.
Do they accept light grudgingly?
I don't think so.

To Fire

You came to me one December morning.
You taught me how to live with nothing,
you old nothing-maker.

You are all consumption and digestion.
You are heat, wind, and embers,
but I didn't get that close.

When I left home that day, my life
was as buoyant as a fish in water.
When I returned there was no normal.

I don't know how to
finish this story. Maybe
I never will.

We can't live together but I can't live apart.
I rely on you, being, as I am,
made of plants that are made of you.

And I like to warm my bones in winter.
But sometimes
you're a little close for comfort.

Stick to the sky, please Friend,
or in the hearth behind closed doors.
I want to love you from a distance.

Lessons from Birds and Butterflies

I intend to write about joy, about light-heartedness, about fun.
Who was it who said, 'There can be no more poetry'?
It was after Auschwitz. These days
many young people don't even know about Auschwitz.
And in between time, it's been atrocity upon atrocity.
Don't give me justifications. It's atrocities all the way.

So it's a bit damn hard to write about joy
while others suffer. Not just the people in terror
while their lives are bombed to pieces,
but people coming home to houses full of mud.
Others clean up after fire, mud slides, melting ice.

I've had my share of suffering.
I know the upsides and, certainly, the down.
But I am here and how am I to find my way
to a life worth living? To witness suffering
but put my nose to a flower?

Today, outside my window, a parrot stood on a stump
and picked dandelion seed heads with his feet
and ate the seeds.
Earlier, a flock of small birds that I've never seen before
sipped nectar from this same patch of weeds.
How can I call them weeds when birds sup?

I guess the point is, despite our weight of loss,
we have to take what's here, and we must let it nourish us.
We must fill our bellies and our hearts with
whatever is at hand. We must put our noses to flowers.

All summer the insects have been doing their thing.
And now butterflies break their way from chrysalises.
Not long ago they were soup.
They pump their crumpled wings into beauty
and open them to the sky, fly hither and yon,
mate, lay eggs, and die.

In the meantime, beauty.
In the meantime, how does it feel to be a butterfly?
What is the nature of joy?

Goldfinches in Dandelions

Where once were red-browed finches and kangaroo grass
European goldfinches feed in the dandelions.
Am I happy about that or sad?
Before, after, then, now, division, comparison. But tell me
what do the goldfinches feel with their
little bodies lively with seed, and their delight
of air and plant and each other.
The world has changed and so have I.
I sow kangaroo grass and plan for red-browed finches
but I delight in dandelions and my heart flutters
with these little winged balls of life.
Doesn't yours?

Black Cockies

The black cockies fly across the sky, crying.
The sound is like sadness, but they hold nothing
of sadness. In this moment they have
no fear. They do not think about the time
of the great fire, when they rose on the winds
beating wings
to fly before the horror.
They do not hold that in their minds
like amulets.

No. They stretch and contract
the muscles of their wings moving through space
on winds that are bigger than them.
And they call to each other in voices that seem sad
but are of this moment.
'Pine!' they say, or 'Hakea!' and they
alight on the plants that give them sustenance.
They do not carry fear or sadness or grief or anger.
They only carry desire for full bellies and for each other.
They only carry weather and their own bodies beating air.

An Ordinary Morning

Suddenly the sun slides up and the world is painted
through red, through orange, through yellow

Soon white light will give us colour
but for now I'll bathe in golden

The grass, the fur of rabbits, even
the black tree-skeletons on the ridge

all golden and better
than the heavy metal

This gold is filled with air like diamonds
and birdsong like jewels

It opens the cage of my chest
Gold in there, gold all the way through

Two years and three months since

perfect
a dandelion seed head
— deep breath

Two years and three months since the fire and everything is ok with my life. But I am not yet rid of this strange breathing tic, nor the associated pain. That's trauma for you. It probably doesn't help that I keep signing myself up to write poetry for my community, and agreeing to do visual arts exhibitions. But if I didn't do that, you wouldn't be reading this, and I wouldn't be taking the opportunity to put a line under it all.

You may have noticed in the last few poems that I'm trying to write about light-hearted things. It's a tall order for me, because I seem to need the contrast of light and dark in every poem that I write!

Many in our community are ready to try to make our lives more multidimensional, but spare a thought for the many in this fireground, and across Australia, who are still in the midst of trying to recover a semblance of normality. And recently there were massive floods that displaced another multitude of people. And a war! So I end this book with a prayerful hope that we humans will find a way to be healthy and humane, and to celebrate good times, together again, on a healthy planet.

every little bit of beauty
I take it for my heart
— the kiss of the wind

And for you, Dear Reader, one last poem:

Why Choose to Dance, Grandma?

My child, there is nothing else
to be done about the world
and its horrors.
There is war here, drought there,
There's flood and fire and famine
and there's not a lot that you and I
can do about it. But when
there is something we can do,
we had better be ready.

How can we stay ready when
each day the plight of others
and ourselves
settles in our gut like stones?
We can suffer it, let it weaken us,
bind us, eat us whole.
Or we can dance.

We can dance and we can sing
and we can draw the good
energy of the earth and the wide sky
into ourselves, fill ourselves
with joy and love
and that's how
we can stay ready.

Lightning Source UK Ltd.
Milton Keynes UK
UKHW020627250722
406332UK00010B/1097